Publisher's Note

IN THE MID-NINETEENTH CENTURY, no household was complete without an abundant supply of lavishly embroidered bed linens, table linens, handkerchiefs, lingerie, shirts, blouses and other items. Often, such embroidery consisted of names, monograms and initials, further embellished with flowers, vines and leaves. Some of the work was undoubtedly done by the ladies of the house—a thorough knowledge of handwork was a part of the education of every lady—but it might also be done by the manufacturers of the goods or by companies or individuals specializing in fancy embroidery. In this latter case, the designs would be chosen by the customer from a catalog or sample book.

The designs in this book were selected from a pair of rare mid-nineteenth-century Spanish volumes of hand-drawn embroidery patterns. Little is known of their origin, but from the number and variety of the designs, and the fact that many of them were marked with what appear to be price and style notations, it seems likely that these volumes were part of such a catalog.

Whatever their history, the grace and beauty of the designs is undeniable, and their appeal is as strong today as it was more than a century ago. Not only are the initials and monograms usable as is—while perhaps not every possible monogram is included, there is certainly a wide selection—but the intricate floral frames and embellishments can be used independently as well.

The designs were originally intended for embroidery, but their usefulness is by no means restricted to that medium. The motifs can be used for fabric painting, tole work, wood painting and burning and many other crafts and is also a rich source of copyright free designs for graphic artists and designers.

Dover would like to express our appreciation to Joslin Hall Rare Books for allowing us to reproduce these pages.

B.R.

ROSALJNA.

D.M.

ILL.R.

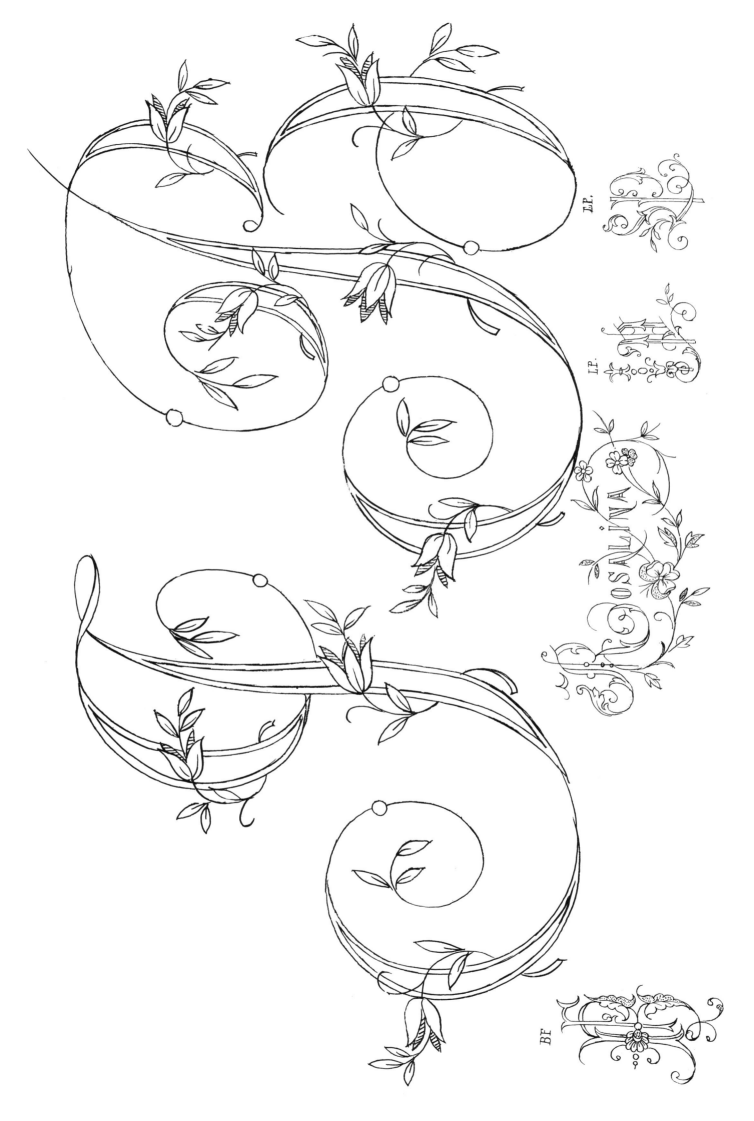

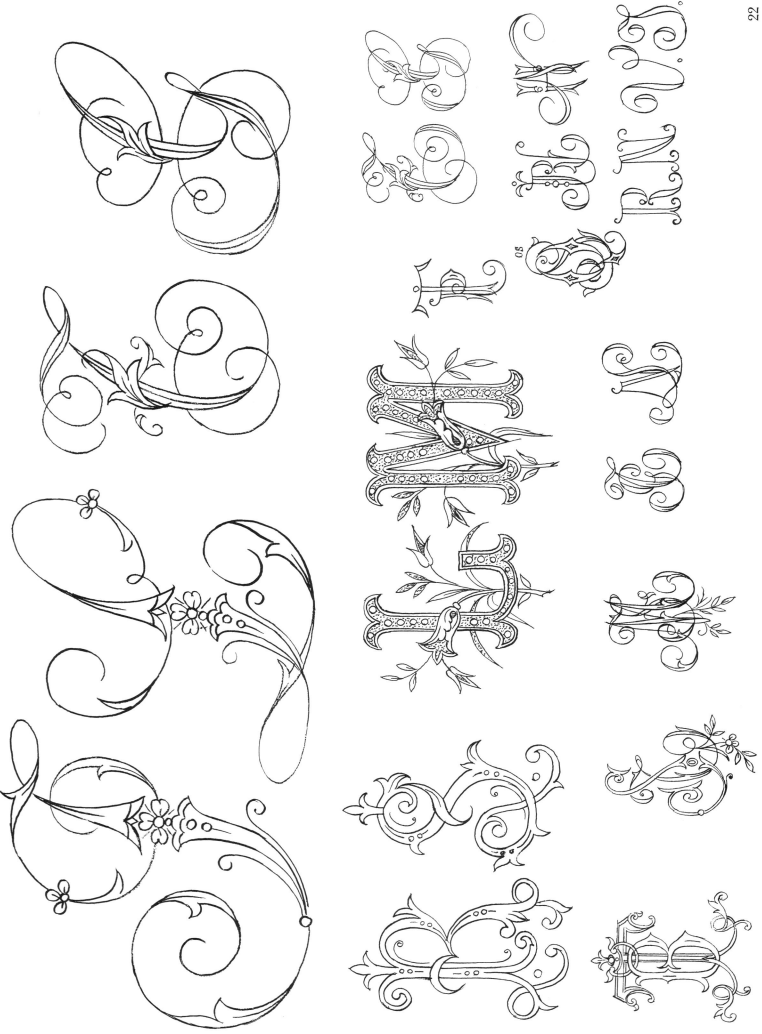

TS

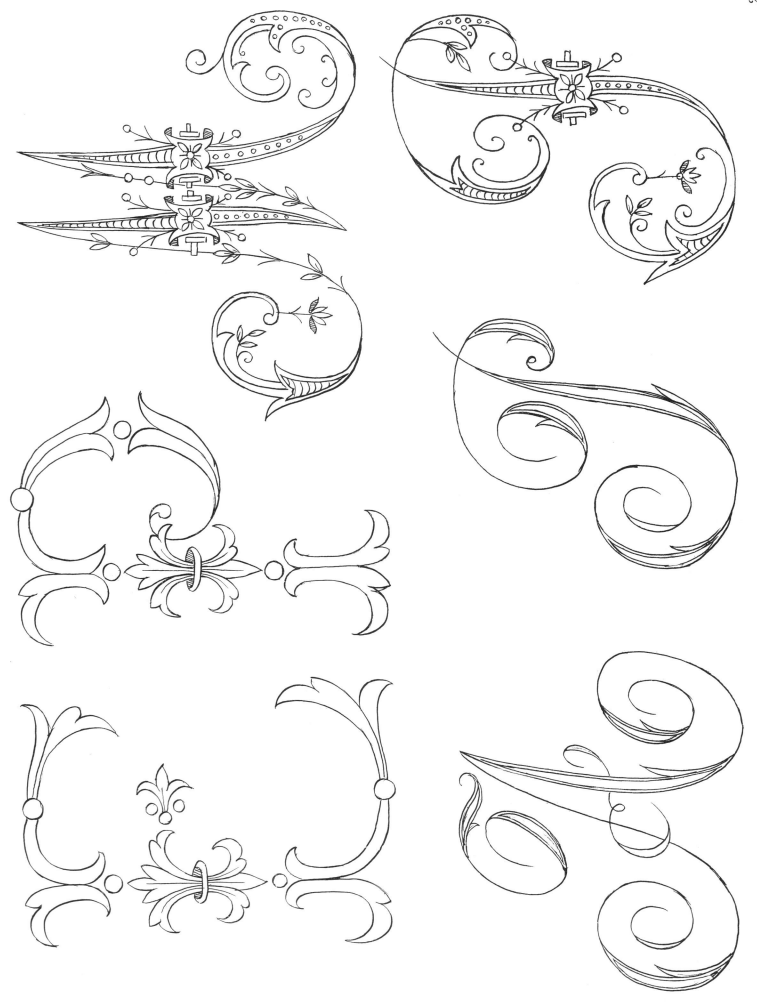

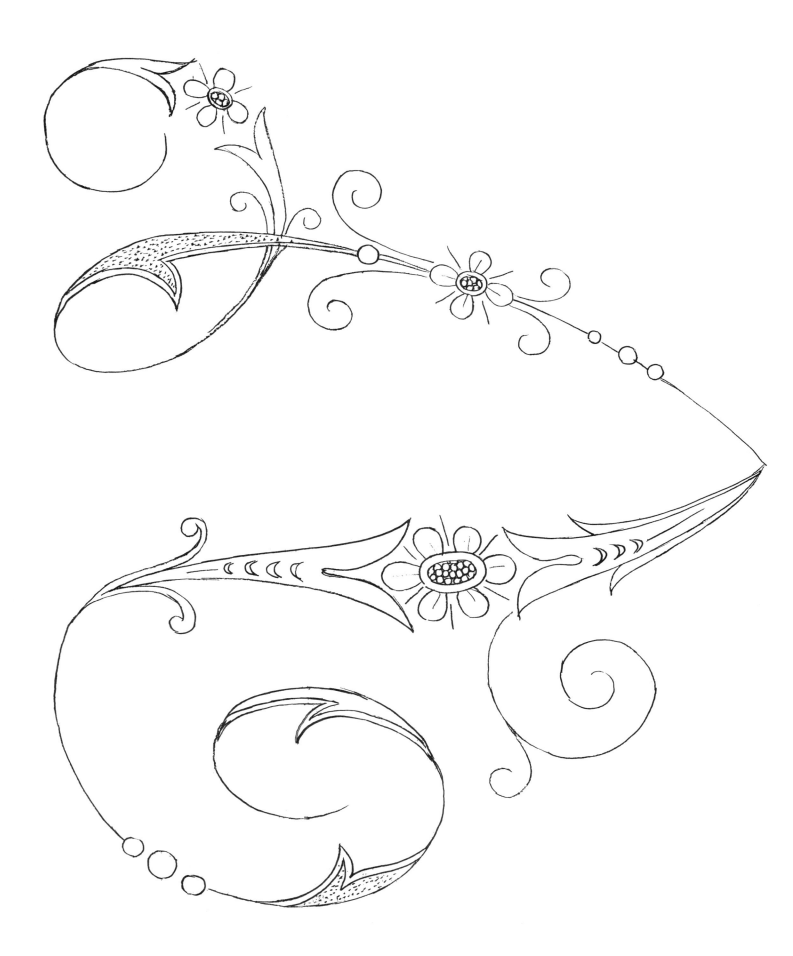

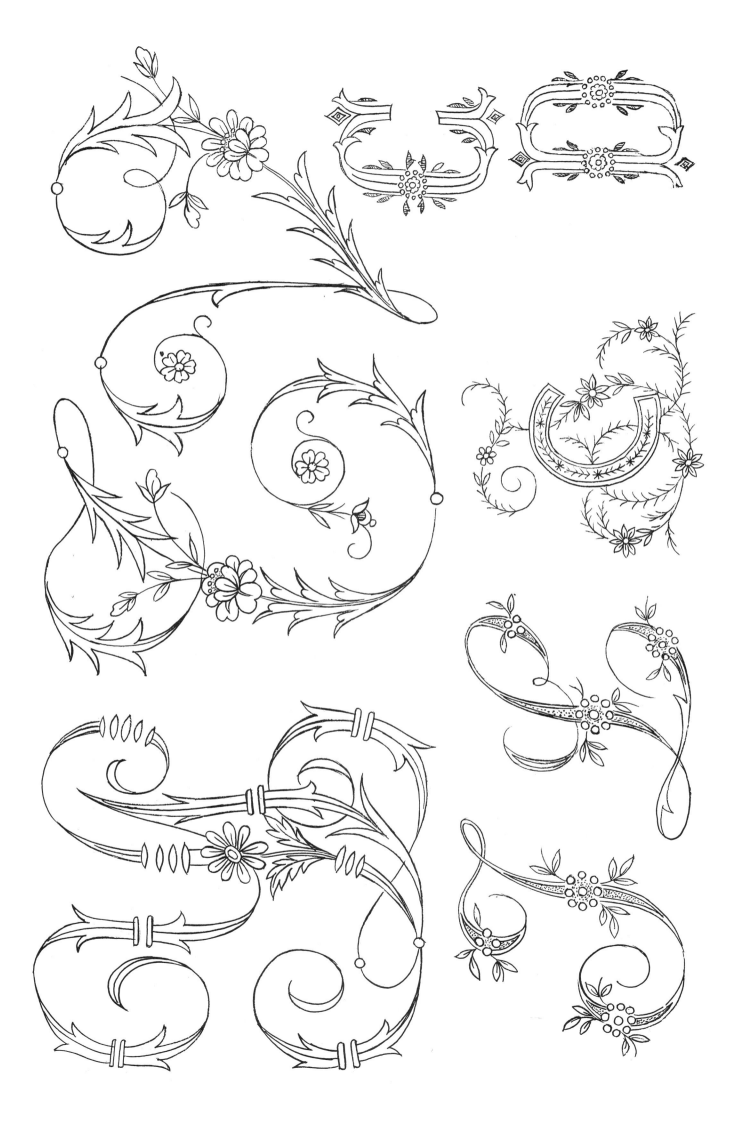

PJ

TG

VC

F.B.

RS

CP

A

BC

GF

IV.

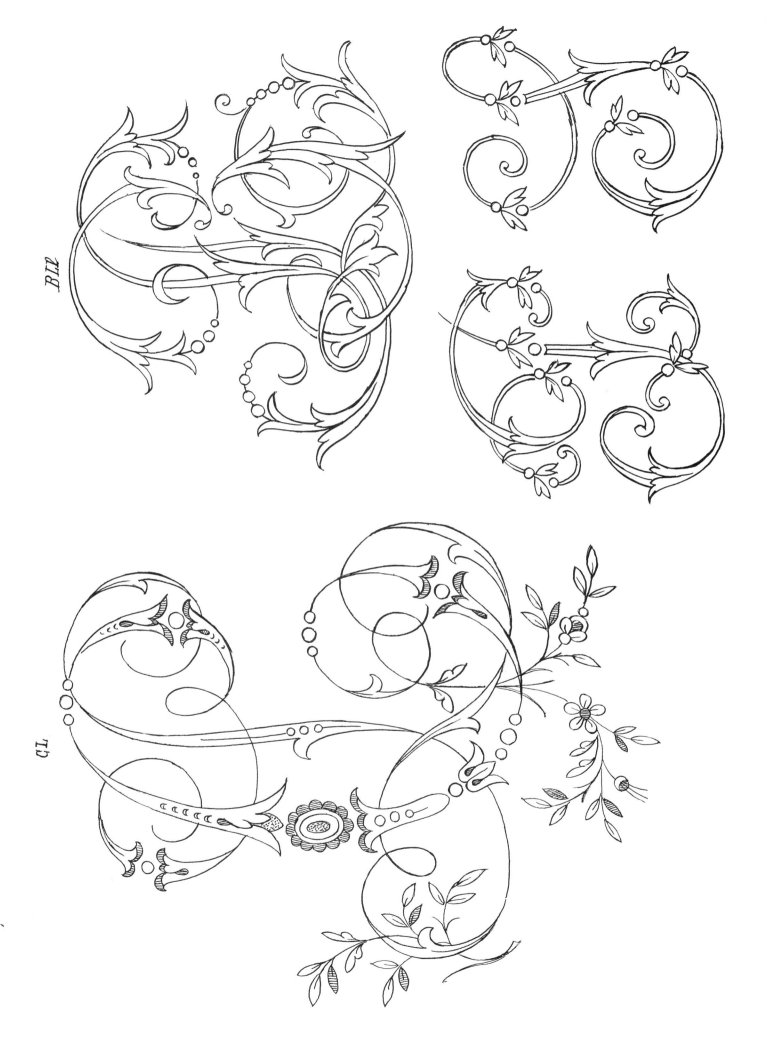

RS

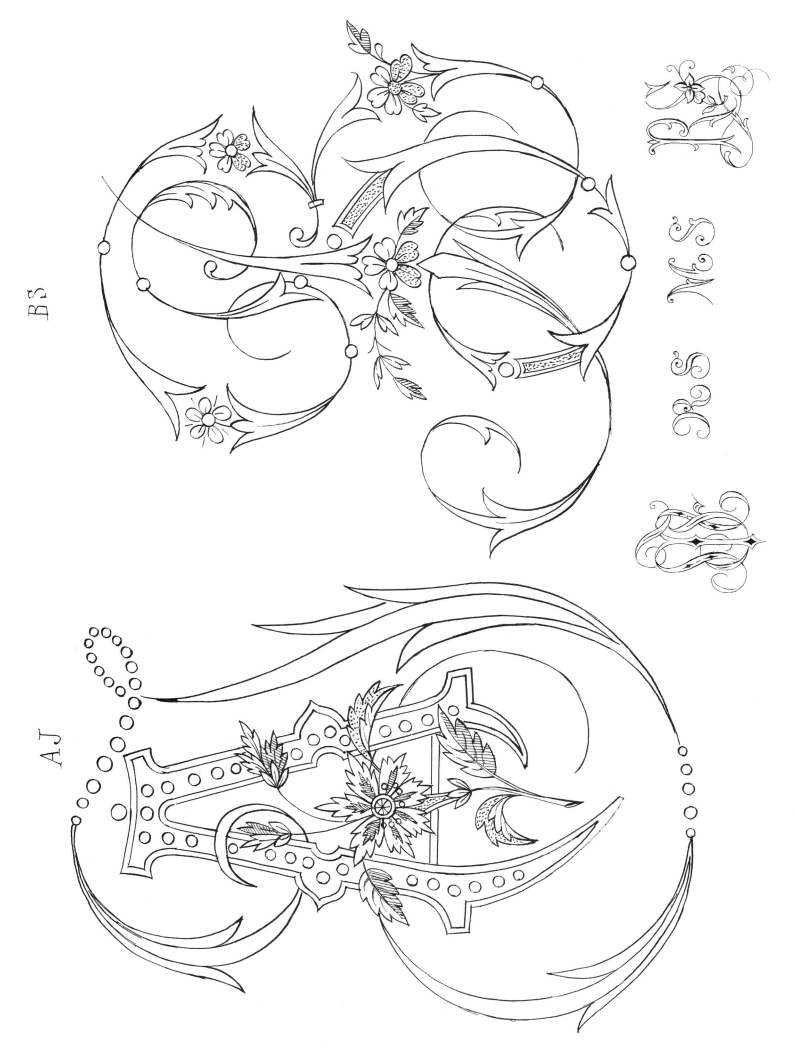

AL

BE

BE

M.G.

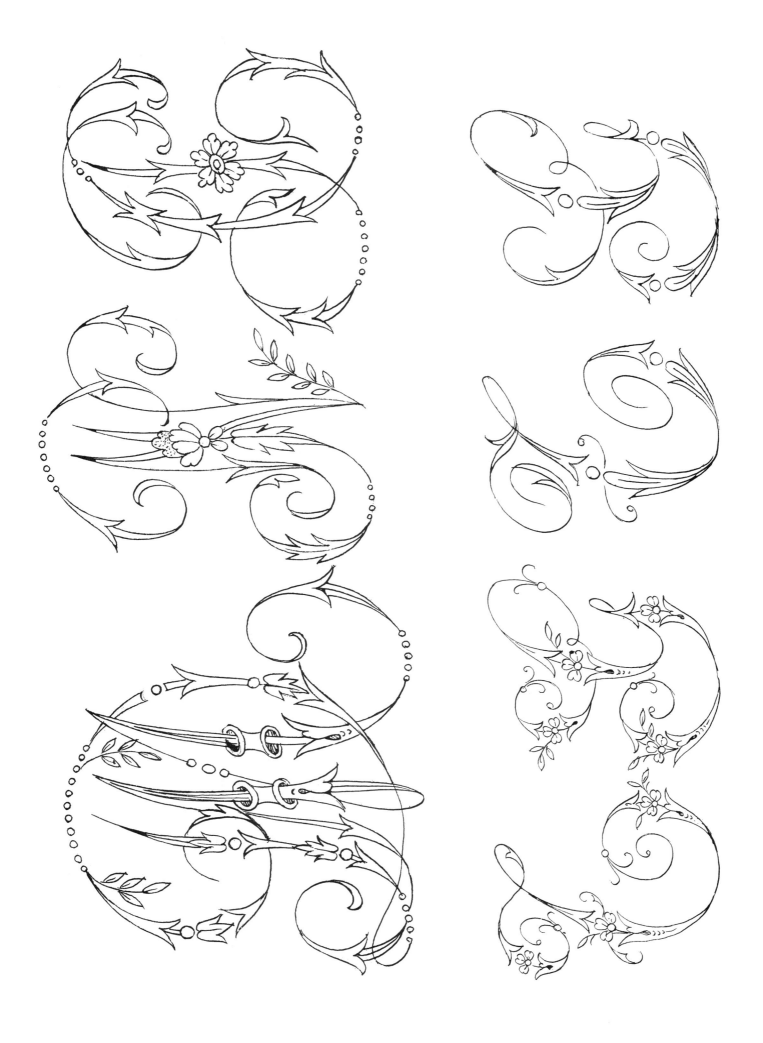

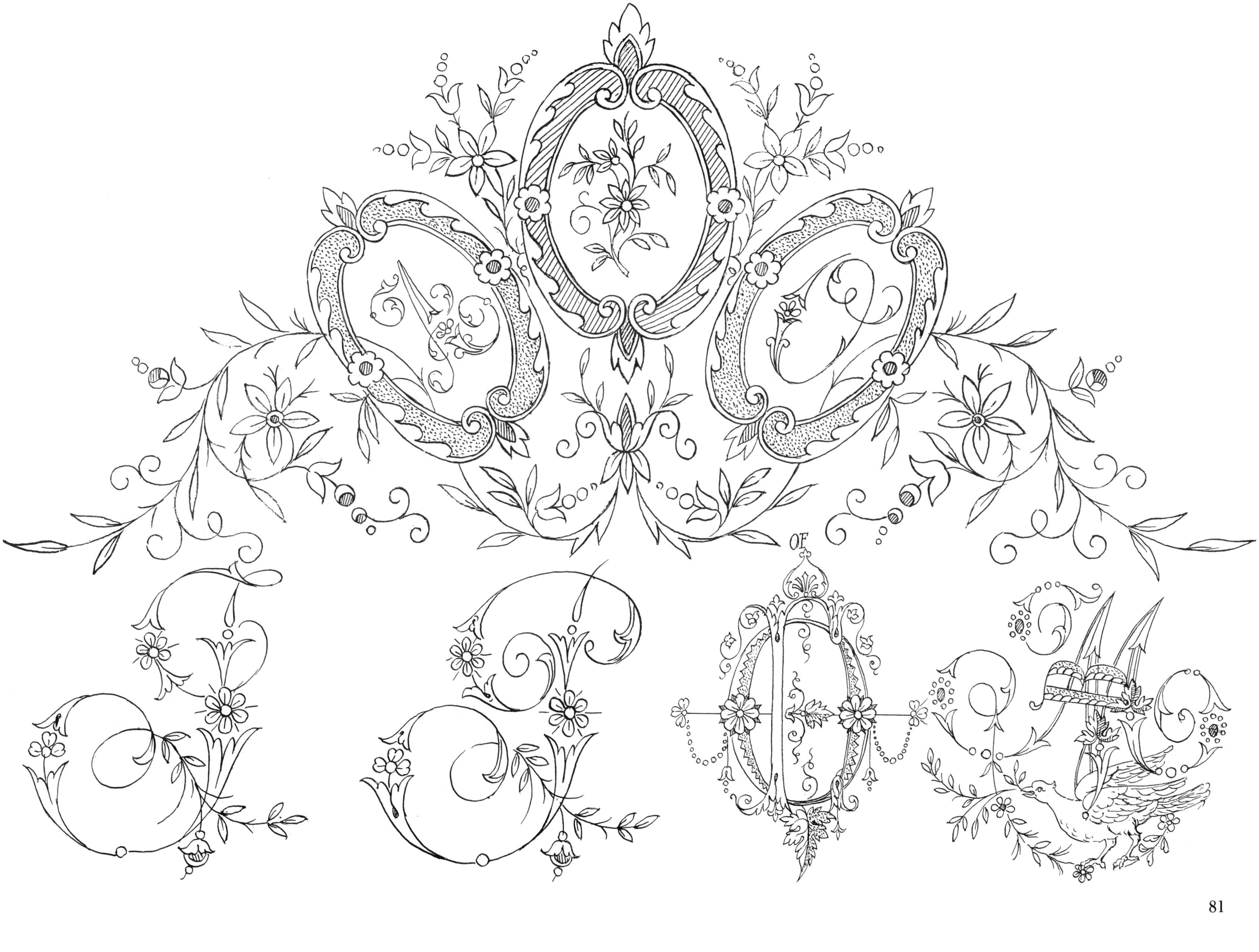

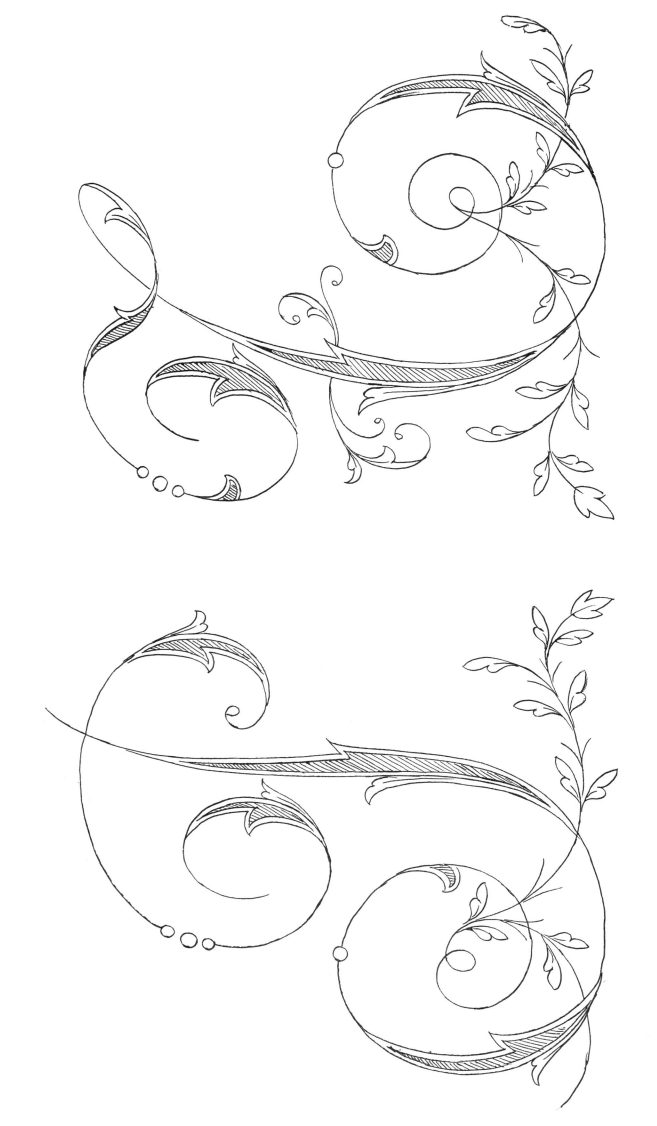

R.D
AP

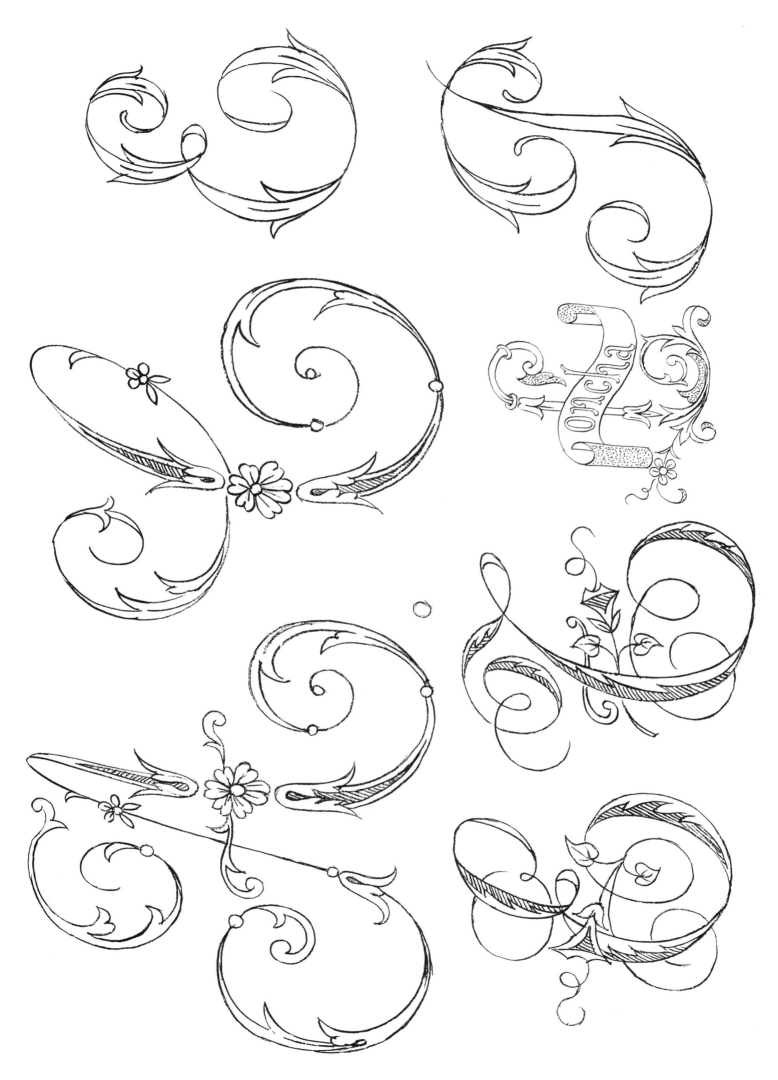

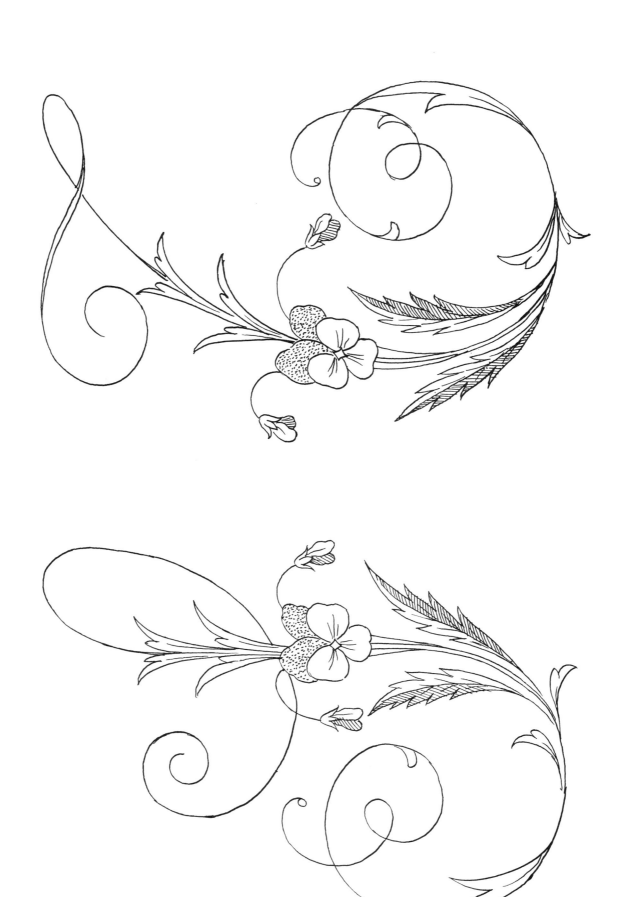

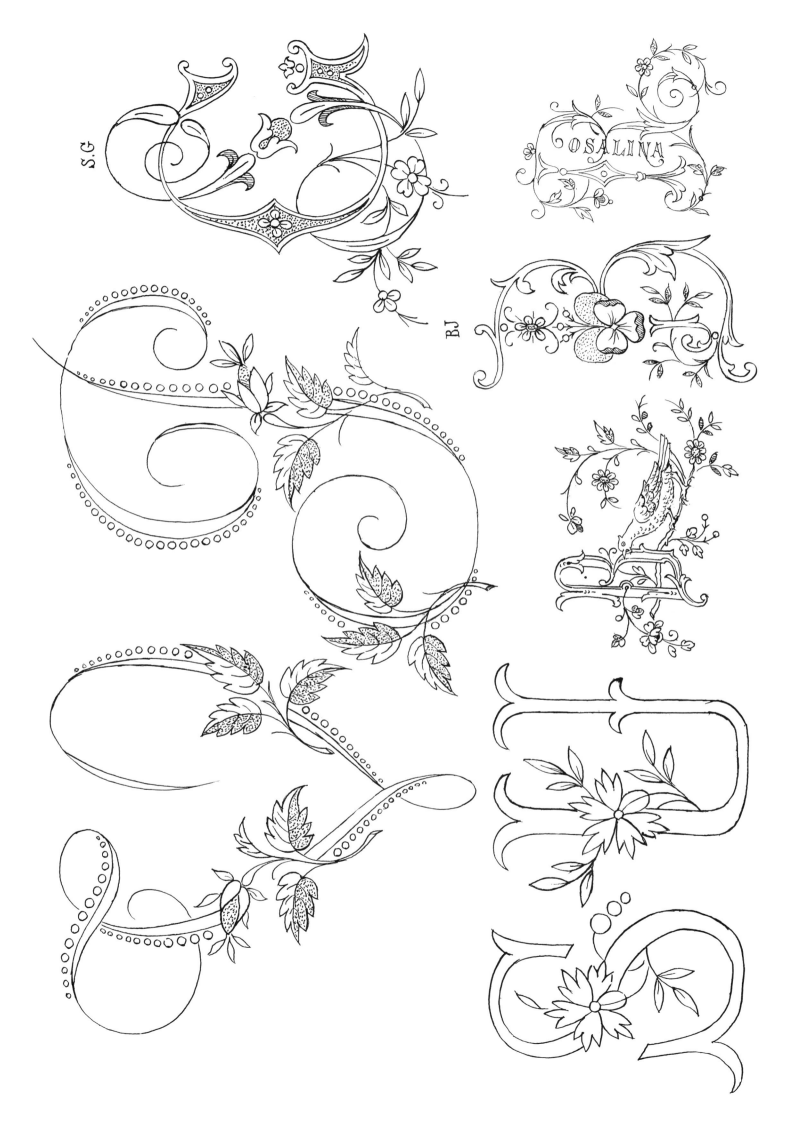

ROSALINE

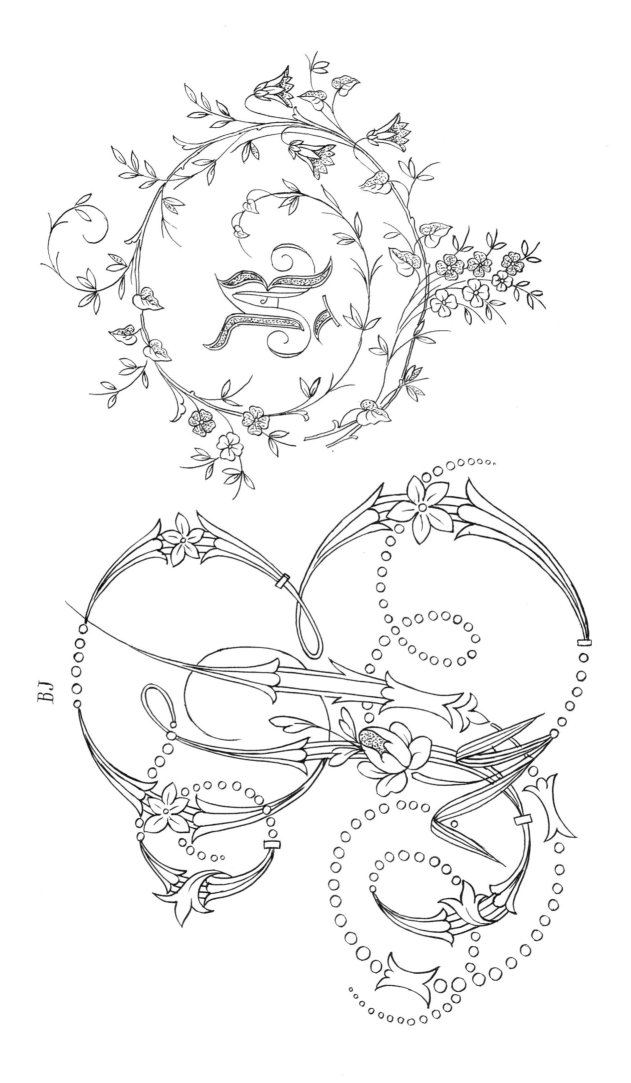

BJ